First hundred words in Italian

Heather Amery

Illustrated by Stephen Cartwright

Translation and pronunciation guide by
Giovanna Iannaco and Loredana Riu

Designed by Mike Olley and Jan McCafferty

There is a little yellow duck to find in every picture.

Il soggiorno The living room

il papà
Daddy

la mamma
Mummy

il bambino
boy

2

la bambina
girl

il bebè
baby

il cane
dog

il gatto
cat

3

I vestiti Clothes

le scarpe
shoes

le mutande
pants

il maglione
jumper

la canottiera
vest

i pantaloni
trousers

la maglietta
t-shirt

i calzini
socks

La colazione Breakfast

il pane
bread

il latte
milk

le uova
eggs

la mela
apple

l'arancia
orange

la banana
banana

La cucina The kitchen

la tavola
table

la sedia
chair

il piatto
plate

il coltello
knife

la forchetta
fork

il cucchiaio
spoon

la tazza
cup

I giocattoli Toys

il cavallo
horse

la pecora
sheep

la mucca
cow

la gallina
hen

il maiale
pig

il treno
train

i cubi
blocks

La visita   The visit

la nonna
Granny

il nonno
Grandpa

le pantofole
slippers

12

il cappotto
coat

il vestito
dress

il cappello
hat

Il parco The park

l'albero
tree

il fiore
flower

le altalene
swings

la palla
ball

lo scivolo
slide

gli stivali
boots

l'uccello
bird

la barca
boat

15

La strada The street

la macchina
car

la bicicletta
bicycle

l'aereo
plane

il furgone
truck

l'autobus
bus

la casa
house

La festa   The party

il palloncino
balloon

la torta
cake

l'orologio
clock

il gelato
ice cream

il pesce
fish

i biscotti
biscuits

le caramelle
sweets

19

La piscina

The swimming pool

il braccio

arm

la mano

hand

la gamba

leg

i piedi
feet

le dita
dei piedi
toes

la testa
head

il sedere
bottom

21

Lo spogliatoio
The changing room

la bocca
mouth

gli occhi
eyes

le orecchie
ears

il naso
nose

i capelli
hair

il pettine
comb

la spazzola
brush

Il negozio <small>The shop</small>

rosso
red

azzurro
blue

verde
green

giallo
yellow

rosa
pink

bianco
white

nero
black

Il bagno The bathroom

il sapone
soap

l'asciugamano
towel

il gabinetto
toilet

la vasca
bath

la pancia
tummy

l'anatra
duck

La camera da letto The bedroom

il letto
bed

la lampada
lamp

la finestra
window

la porta
door

il libro
book

la bambola
doll

l'orsacchiotto
teddy

Match the words to the pictures

l'anatra

l'arancia

la bambola

la banana

i calzini

il cane

la canottiera

il cappello

il coltello

la finestra

la forchetta

il gatto

il gelato

la lampada

il latte

il libro

la macchina

il maglione

il maiale

la mela

la mucca

l'orologio

l'orsacchiotto

la palla

il pesce

gli stivali

la tavola

la torta

il treno

l'uovo

I numeri Numbers

1 **uno/una**
one

2 **due**
two

3 **tre**
three

4 **quattro**
four

5 **cinque**
five

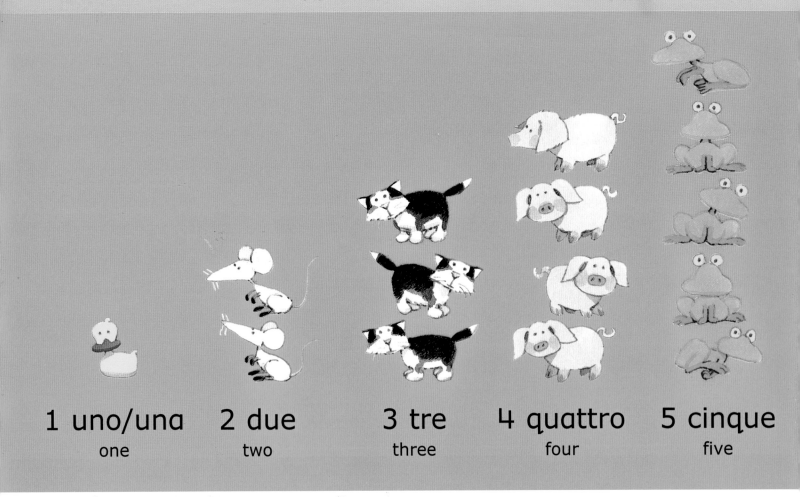

1 **uno/una**
one

2 **due**
two

3 **tre**
three

4 **quattro**
four

5 **cinque**
five

Word list

In this alphabetical list of all the words in the pictures, the Italian word comes first, next is the guide to saying the word, and then there is the English translation. The guide may look strange or funny, but just try to read the words as if they were English. It will help you to say the words in Italian correctly, if you remember these rules:

c before *e* or *i* is said like *ch* in *cheese*

ch before *e* or *i* is said like *k* in *king*

gh before *e* or *i* is said like *g* as in *get*

sc before *e* or *i* is said like *sh* in *shop*

z is said like *ts* in *cats*.

Most Italian words have a part that you stress, or say louder (like the "day" part of the English word "today").

So you know which part of each word you should stress, it is shown in letters **like this** in the pronunciation guide. In the guide:

ay is said like *a* in d*a*te

o is said like *o* in h*o*t

ow is said like *ow* in c*ow*

e is said like *e* in ten even when it is followed by *r*, so *per* sounds like *pear* not like the *per* in pro*per*

ly is said like *lli* in bri*lli*ant

ny is said like the *ni* in o*ni*on

r is always sounded; try rolling it a little, *rrr;*

g is said like the *g* in *g*et

s is always said like the *s* in *s*et

l'aereo (m)	*la-**ay**rayo*	plane
l'albero (m)	***lal**bairo*	tree
le altalene	*lay alta**lay**nay*	swings
l'anatra (f)	***la**natra*	duck
l'arancia (f)	*la**ran**cha*	orange
l'asciugamano (m)	*lashooga**ma**no*	towel
l'autobus (m)	***low**toboos*	bus
azzurro	*a**tzoo**rro*	blue
il bagno	*eel **ban**yo*	bathroom
la bambina	*la bam**bee**na*	girl
il bambino	*eel bam**bee**no*	boy
la bambola	*la **bam**bola*	doll
la banana	*la ba**na**na*	banana
la barca	*la **bar**ka*	boat
il bebè	*eel be**bay***	baby
bianco	***byan**co*	white
la bicicletta	*la beechee**klet**ta*	bicycle
i biscotti	*ee bee**skot**tee*	biscuits
la bocca	*la **bok**ka*	mouth
il braccio	*eel **bra**cho*	arm
i calzini	*ee kal**tzee**nee*	socks
la camera da letto	*la **kam**aira da **let**to*	bedroom
il cane	*eel **ka**nay*	dog
la canottiera	*la kanot**tyair**a*	vest
i capelli	*ee ka**pel**lee*	hair
il cappello	*eel kap**pel**lo*	hat
il cappotto	*eel kap**pot**to*	coat
le caramelle	*lay kara**mel**lay*	sweets
la casa	*la **ka**za*	house
il cavallo	*eel ka**val**lo*	horse
cinque	***cheen**kway*	five
la colazione	*la kolat**zeeo**nay*	breakfast
il coltello	*eel kol**tel**lo*	knife
i cubi	*ee **koo**bee*	blocks
il cucchiaio	*eel kook**kya**eeo*	spoon
la cucina	*la koo**chee**na*	kitchen
le dita dei piedi	*lay **dee**ta day **pye**dee*	toes
due	***doo**ay*	two
la festa	*la **fes**ta*	party
la finestra	*la fee**nes**tra*	window
il fiore	*eel **fyor**ee*	flower
la forchetta	*la for**ket**ta*	fork
il furgone	*eel foor**go**nay*	truck
il gabinetto	*eel gabee**net**to*	toilet
la gallina	*la gal**lee**na*	hen

33

la gamba	la **gam**ba	leg
il gatto	eel **gat**to	cat
il gelato	eel je**la**to	ice cream
giallo	**jal**lo	yellow
i giocattoli	ee jo**kat**tolee	toys
la lampada	la **lam**pada	lamp
il latte	eel **lat**tay	milk
il letto	eel **let**to	bed
il libro	eel **lee**bro	book
la macchina	la **mak**keena	car
la maglietta	la ma**lyet**ta	t-shirt
il maglione	eel ma**lyon**ay	jumper
il maiale	eel ma**ya**lay	pig
la mamma	la **mam**ma	Mummy
la mano	la **ma**no	hand
la mela	la **may**la	apple
la mucca	la **moo**kka	cow
le mutande	lay moo**tan**day	pants
il naso	eel **na**zo	nose
il negozio	eel ne**got**syo	shop
nero	**nair**o	black
la nonna	la **non**na	Granny
il nonno	eel **non**no	Grandpa
i numeri	ee **noo**mairee	numbers
gli occhi	lyee **ok**kee	eyes
le orecchie	lay o**rek**kyay	ears
l'orologio (m)	loro**lo**jo	clock
l'orsacchiotto	lorsak**kyot**to	teddy
la palla	la **pal**la	ball
il palloncino	eel pallon**chee**no	balloon
la pancia	la **pan**cha	tummy
il pane	eel **pa**nay	bread
i pantaloni	ee panta**lo**nee	trousers
le pantofole	lay pan**to**folay	slippers
il papà	eel pa**pa**	Daddy
il parco	eel **par**ko	park
la pecora	la **pay**cora	sheep
il pesce	eel **pe**shay	fish
il pettine	eel **pet**teenay	comb
il piatto	eel **pyat**to	plate
i piedi	ee **pye**dee	feet
la piscina	la pee**schee**na	swimming pool
la porta	la **por**ta	door
quattro	**kwat**tro	four
rosa	**ro**za	pink
rosso	**ros**so	red
il sapone	eel sap**on**ay	soap
le scarpe	lay **skar**pay	shoes
lo scivolo	lo **shee**volo	slide
il sedere	eel se**dair**ay	bottom
la sedia	la **se**dya	chair
il soggiorno	eel soj**jor**no	living room
la spazzola	la **spat**tsola	brush
lo spogliatoio	lo spolya**to**yo	changing room
gli stivali	lyee stee**va**lee	boots
la strada	la **stra**da	street
la tavola	la **tav**ola	table
la tazza	la **tat**tsa	cup
la testa	la **tes**ta	head
la torta	la **tor**ta	cake
tre	**tray**	three
il treno	eel **tray**no	train
l'uccello (m)	loo**chel**lo	bird
uno (m) / una (f)	**oo**no / **oo**na	one
le uova	lay **wo**va	eggs
l'uovo (m)	**lwo**vo	egg
la vasca	la **vas**ka	bath
verde	**vair**day	green
i vestiti	ee ves**tee**tee	clothes
il vestito	eel ves**tee**to	dress
la visita	la **vee**seeta	visit

First published in 2008 by Usborne Publishing Ltd, Usborne House, 83-85 Saffron Hill, London EC1N 8RT, England. www.usborne.com Copyright © 2008 Usborne Publishing Ltd.